THE HARLEY STREET COOK B

The Favourite Recipes of the Harley Street and Regional Professionals

Edited by
Gloria Rowbotham

THE HARLEY STREET COOK BOOK

THE FAVOURITE RECIPES OF THE HARLEY STREET AND REGIONAL PROFESSIONALS

EDITED BY

GLORIA ROWBOTHAM

TIFFANY PUBLISHERS

First published in the United Kingdom in 1995
Tiffany Publishers Limited

ISBN 1 899014 00 4

Printed by Chandlers Printers Limited, Saxon Mews, Reginald Road,
Bexhill-on-Sea, East Sussex, TN39 3PJ, England.

Illustrations and design by Julian Abela Hyzler.

Many thanks to Allan Wallace for his indispensable help in editing this
book.

CONTENTS

Editor's Note   6

A History of Harley Street   7

Starters   8

Main Courses   46

Desserts   98

Cocktails   134

Appendix   142

Editor's Note

I have had great pleasure in compiling this unique book. My very special thanks go to those on Harley Street and the region, who, despite their extremely busy schedules, have taken the time to donate their favourite recipes to this book.

Donations will be made from the proceeds of this book to the Help the Hospices. This charity cares for the terminally ill and their families by providing in patient beds and home care. Money is needed to support the training of nurses, doctors and all who work in hospices in the special skills that are unique to hospice care. Total Care is involved in the care of the elderly and will also benefit from the sales. I hope that you will have as much pleasure in using the recipes from this book as I have had in compiling it!

The History of Harley Street

Harley Street is renowned internationally for its medical specialists. First rated in 1753, Harley Street was named after its ground landlord, Edward Harley, the 2nd Earl of Oxford. Harley Street was a fashionable residential area before the doctors began to practice on the street in the mid 19th century. Some of the more noted personalities who lived on the street included Kitty, the Duchess of Wellington who lived at number 11 in 1809-14, Turner who lived at number 64 in 1804-8 and Gladstone who lived at number 73 in 1876.

There were only 19 doctors in the region in 1858. By the turn of the century, this number had increased to 157. The reason why Harley Street and the region became a medical area is not known. Amongst the many renowned members of the medical profession who have practised on Harley Street and the region were Sir Morell Mackenzie who practised at number 19, Sir Frederick Treves at number 6 Wimpole Street, Sir James Mackenzie at number 33 and Sir Bertrand Dawson at 32 Wimpole Street. This list is by no means exhaustive, a full consideration being beyond the scope of this book.

starters

scampi with pernod

Miss Marianne Vandendriessche FRCS

Ingredients:

600 g (21 oz) of scampi (without shell)
250 g (9 oz) shrimps
¼ l (9 fl oz) cream
350 g (12 ½ oz) mushrooms
1 soupspoon tomato purée
1 onion, finely chopped
1 to 3 soupspoons Pernod
1/4 l (9 fl oz) bisque de homard (1 tin)
butter for frying

Method:

Roll the scampi in flour and then bake in butter. When half cooked, add the onions and mushrooms. Add the shrimps at the end of cooking. Flambé with Pernod. Add the bisque de homard and tomato purée. Cook for a few minutes. Add the cream and bring to the boil. Serve warm with rice.

salmon mouse

Dr Maurice Nellen

Ingredients: serves 4

1 lb (450 g) tomatoes
1 onion, finely chopped
3 tablespoons mayonnaise
1 large tin of salmon
2 level dessertspoons powdered gelatine
margarine for frying
salt
ground black pepper

Method:

Skin the tomatoes by placing in boiling water for 30 seconds and then peeling off
the skin. Chop the tomatoes into small pieces. Finely chop the onions. Add the
tomatoes and fry in margarine for 10 minutes. Purée the mixture by passing
through a sieve. Add the mayonnaise and salmon — taking care to remove bones
and skin — to this purée and mix well, adding salt and pepper to taste. Dissolve
the gelatine powder in 3 tablespoons of hot water and add to the mixture. Spread
a layer of mayonnaise at the bottom of a mould and place the mixture into this
mould over the mayonnaise. Chill overnight.

courgette and almond soup

Dr Edmondson

Ingredients:

2 oz (50 g) flaked almonds
1 oz (25 g) unsalted butter
1 shallot - peeled and finely chopped
½ clove of garlic - chopped
¼ level teaspoon curry powder
1 lb (450 g) courgettes - sliced
1 ¼ pints (700 ml) chicken stock
5 fl. oz (140 ml) single cream
¼ level teaspoon nutmeg
¼ level teaspoon cinnamon
toasted flaked almonds for the garnish

Method:

Boil the flaked almonds in salted water for 30 seconds; drain and dry. Melt the butter and sweat the onion and garlic until transparent. Add the curry powder and cook for 1 minute. Add the sliced courgettes - stirring constantly. Add the boiled almonds and chicken stock and simmer for 20 minutes. Then add the cream and boil for a further 5 minutes. Add the nutmeg, cinnamon, salt and pepper to taste. Blend using a blender and then sieve. Crush the toasted almonds slightly and sprinkle on the top.

hedgehogs

Dr Maurice Nellen

Ingredients:

cooked peeled prawns
béchamel sauce - very thick (see appendix)
parsley or dill - finely chopped
vermicelli

Method:

Mix the cooked prawns, dill or parsley with the very thick bechamel sauce and refrigerate until solid. Roll into small balls and dip into crushed raw vermicelli. Deep fry. Serve with mustarda di frutti (a condiment of dried fruits in a mustard sauce) or chutney.

sunny chicken salad

This recipe is perfect for a hot summer day.

Dr C M E Rowland Payne

Ingredients:

1 ½ lbs (680 g) skinless chicken breasts
2 cups chopped celery.

<u>Sauce:</u>
½ cup mayonnaise
2 tablespoons lemon juice
1 level teaspoon seasoned salt
¼ cup chopped sweet pickle
black pepper

Method:

Simmer the chicken breasts in water for about 40 minutes. Let them cool, and then cut and dice them. This should make about 3 cups of diced cooked chicken. Mix the chicken and celery together in a bowl. Mix all the sauce ingredients in a separate bowl and add this to the chicken and celery, mixing well. Refrigerate for at least 1 hour.

salmon and avocado terrine

Dr Edmondson

Ingredients:

8 oz (225 g) smoked salmon trimmings
5 shallots
2 level tablespoons spring onions, chopped
white pepper
¾ pt (430 ml) double cream
4 oz (115 g) unsalted butter
2 large avocados
juice of one lemon

Garnish:
sour cream
watercress sprigs
sliced lemon

Method:

Blend the salmon, shallots, spring onions, butter, pepper and lemon juice in a blender until thick and smooth. Fold in the cream. Peel and cut the avocado into slices. Line a 2 lb (1 kg) loaf tin with greaseproof paper. Fill it with alternate layers of the mixture and the sliced avocado. Leave in the fridge for 5 hours. To serve, turn out and slice. Serve with a little sour cream, and garnish with a sprig of watercress and a slice of lemon.

smoked salmon pate

Mr Harvey White

Ingredients:

10 oz (300 g) smoked salmon
3 oz (85 g) melted butter
2 oz (55 g) double cream
salt, black pepper
lots of lemon juice

Method:

Liquidize all the ingredients, adjust seasoning and refrigerate. You can use ends of smoked salmon from your friendly neighbourhood fishmonger.

pitta pizzas

This is my favourite tea time snack, but could be used as a starter

Mr Julian Shah FRCS

Ingredients: serves 2

2 pitta breads
butter and/or mayonnaise
4 tomatoes, chopped
diced ham or other cold meat
chopped cucumber/lettuce
1 ripe avocado
mozzarella cheese, sliced
basil
cayenne pepper

Method:

Mix together the tomatoes, ham, cucumber and lettuce and any other meat and vegetable leftovers. Add seasoning. Microwave until hot. Cut open the pitta bread, but leave attached on one side. Toast until golden under the grill. Butter, and spread with mayonnaise or ripe avocado. Pile on tomato and ham mixture and cover with sliced mozzarella. Grill until cheese has melted.

shrimps in a lemon tomato and peanut sauce

Dr Gillian M Vanhegan MB BS DRCOG MIPM

Ingredients: serves 6

3 avocados
300 g (10 ½ oz) shrimps
2 tablespoons crunchy peanut butter
juice of one lemon
3 tablespoons water
½ teaspoon chilli powder
sliced tomato for decoration

Method:

Peal and slice the avocados. Arrange with the shrimps on six plates. Heat the rest of the ingredients over a low heat stirring until the sauce thickens. Pour sauce over shrimps and avocado and decorate with tomato slices.

german cucumber salad

Dr M J Kellett

Ingredients:

1-2 cucumbers peeled and thinly sliced
3 tablespoons water
salt
a good pinch of sugar
1 teaspoon white wine vinegar
crushed caraway or dill seeds

Method:

Salt the prepared cucumbers and leave to stand for half an hour. Rinse and drain well. Make a dressing of white wine vinegar and water with a good pinch of sugar and a few crushed seeds. Serve.

cullen skink

Dr J Briggs

Ingredients:

1 piece smoked haddock
1 leek
1 tablespoon butter
½ pint (280 ml) water
12 pint (280 ml) milk
1 potato
parsley and a bay leaf
1 level tablespoon butter
1 level tablespoon flour

Method:

Skink is an old Scots word for a stew soup and Cullen Skink, as the name implies, originated at the fishing town of Cullen on the Moray Firth. Over the years, its fame has spread and it is a popular dish in the East Neuk of Fife where the National Trust for Scotland has been responsible for restoring many of the old houses on the quayside under their 'Little Houses Improvement Scheme'.
Chop up the white of the leek and soften in the butter. Add the haddock in small pieces, the diced potato, bay leaf, milk and water. Bring to the boil and simmer for 20 minutes. Mix the flour and butter together with a fork and then add to the liquid. Bring to the boil, add salt and black pepper, scatter over some chopped parsley and serve.

23

welsh soup

This is a favourite Welsh hearty soup recipe for a cold winter's day.

Mr D M Davies FRCS

Ingredients:

3 lbs (1.4 kg) topside or brisket of beef
1 ounce (50 g) butter or oil
1 large onion, diced
2 large carrots, diced
1 swede, diced
1 stick of celery, chopped
2 large leeks, diced
a few peppercorns
blade of mace
1 bay leaf
salt and pepper to taste
2 level tablespoons chopped parsley

Method:

Use a heavy based pan on top of the stove or a pressure cooker if you have one. Season the meat on all sides and fry in the hot fat or oil until lightly browned all over. Cover with water and bring to the boil, skimming off any froth that rises to the top. Add the peppercorns and the blade of mace. Cover and simmer over gentle heat for about three hours. Alternatively, pressure cook fifteen minutes per pound (35 minutes per kg). Add remaining vegetables except leeks for the final half-hour of cooking or final five minutes if pressure cooking. I like to add the chopped leeks about five minutes before the end so that they retain their bright colour and do not overcook. Check the seasoning and serve the liquid with some of the vegetables as a soup, sprinkled with the parsley. Remove the leeks and serve hot with the rest of the vegetables as a main course. This dish is even more tasty if served the following day when all the flavours have developed.

24

guacamole

A wonderful pre-dinner appetizer and drink.

Dr Edward Stonehill MD FRCPsych

Ingredients:

4 ripe avocados
1 green pepper (de-seeded)
4 tomatoes (peeled)
1 onion
4 cloves of garlic
Bunch of coriander leaves
1 green chilli
juice of 1 lemon
1 teaspoon of sugar
salt & pepper to taste

Method:

Blend all the ingredients in a food mixer and serve as a dip.

lees potatoes

Mr Angus B Gordon

Ingredients:

1 ½ lbs (680 g) even-sized potatoes
3 tablespoons olive oil
1 level teaspoon mustard seeds
1 level teaspoon cumin seeds
2 level tablespoons sesame seeds
cayenne to taste
juice of ½ lemon

Method:

Boil the potatoes in their jackets. Peel when cool and cut into cubes. Heat the oil in a heavy frying pan. Add the mustard seeds and cumin and cook for a minute. Add the potatoes and brown, adding the sesame seeds and the cayenne after a few minutes. Sprinkle with lemon juice and serve hot.

grilled goat's cheese with bacon and walnuts

Mrs Jude Matthews BDS

Ingredients:

1 round of goat's cheese per person
1 head of lettuce
white bread
grapes (seedless)
bacon
walnuts (toasted)
olive oil

Method:

Snip the bacon into small pieces and sauté gently with olive oil and halved grapes. Split the rounds of cheese and place each on a round of toasted white bread. Grill gently till soft and slightly browned, watching all the time to prevent burning. Arrange lettuce leaves on each plate, and place the bread and cheese on top, 2 rounds per person. Cover liberally with the sautéd bacon and grapes, and sprinkle with toasted walnuts. Serve immediately.

baked vegetables

Mr Morgan

Ingredients:

2 red, 2 green and 2 yellow bell peppers
1 onion
1 leek
1 aubergine (any vegetable you like in fact)
6 cloves of garlic
3 tablespoons olive oil
1 tablespoon vinegar
oregano and basil to garnish

Method:

Chop the vegetables, mix them with the other ingredients and place them in a baking tin. Sprinkle with oregano and season to taste. Cook in a pre-heated oven at Gas Mark 6 (400 degrees F/205 degrees C) for half an hour. Turn the vegatables and cook for another half hour. Top with the basil and serve. The timing depends on how you like vegetables — I like them charred at the edges.

coquilles st jacques au beurre blanc

Mr Jonathan Bradbeer

Ingredients:

1 lb (450 g) scallops (without their corals)
salt
freshly ground pepper
4 French shallots, finely chopped
6 tablespoonfuls dry white wine
3 tablespoons white wine vinegar
7 oz (200 g) butter

Method:

Rinse scallops and pat dry. Cut each in half into two thinner discs. Season. Combine shallots, wine, vinegar and salt and pepper in a small saucepan. Simmer gently over a low heat until only 2 teaspoons of liquid remain. Meanwhile cut the butter into ¾ inch (15 mm) cubes, setting aside ¾ oz (20 g). Over a very low heat, vigorously whisk the butter into the saucepan, piece by piece. When all the butter has been incorporated and this 'beurre blanc' is light and foamy, set it aside and keep warm. Melt the remaining butter in a frying pan and coat the scallops over a very low heat for 20 seconds on each side. Divide amongst 4 plates and pour over the sauce. Serve immediately. If preferred, the scallops can be lightly grilled.

champ

Mr A M Hamilton FRCS FRCOphth

Ingredients:

2 lb (900 g) of Irish potatoes
1 bunch of spring onions
¼ pint (140 ml) of milk

Method:

Boil the potatoes for 30 minutes in salted water. Finely chop the spring onions and boil and then simmer for five minutes in the milk. Mash the potatoes and add the milk and spring onions. Place in a serving dish with a large knob of butter on top. Wash down with a glass of buttermilk and a pint of Murphy's.

easy peasy tomato soup

Judith H Graham Secretary to Dr Angus Blair

Ingredients:

1 tin of chopped tomatoes
1 or 2 medium sized onions chopped finely
1 tablespoon of plain flour
1 oz (25 g) butter
1 chicken stock cube mixed with boiling water to the top of a tea cup
1 small tin of evaporated milk
1 small tin of tomato purée mixed with boiling water to ¾ pint (430 ml)
sherry, parsley and cream

Method:

Sauté the onion in the butter for about two minutes. Remove from heat and stir in flour. Add stock, tomato purée, tomatoes and evaporated milk and simmer for about twenty minutes. Just before serving, fling in a dash of sherry (Croft Original is nicest), a teaspoonful of fresh cream and parsley to garnish. Easy Peasy!! Note — if you want to freeze the soup, don't add the sherry and cream.

bacon and mushroom quiche

Mr Michael A Smith

Ingredients:

3 oz (85 g) butter
6 oz (170 g) plain flour

Filling:
6 oz (170 g) back bacon
4 oz (115 g) mushrooms, sliced
3 tomatoes
2 eggs, size 3
½ pint (280 ml) milk
4 tablespoons single cream

Method:

For the pastry, rub the butter into the flour, add some cold water and mix. For the filling, start by chopping the bacon into small pieces and dry-fry until golden. Add the mushrooms and cook until soft. Whisk the eggs, milk and cream together. Pre-heat the oven to 400 degrees F/200 degrees C/Gas Mark 6. Roll out the pastry to line an 8 inch (20 cm) loose-bottomed flan tin (or a flan ring on a baking sheet). Scatter the bacon, mushrooms and sliced tomatoes over the base and pour in the egg mixture. Bake for 15 minutes before reducing the oven to 350 degrees F/180 degrees C/Gas Mark 4 for a further 20-25 minutes.

dolcelatte salad with mango

Mr OJ Gilmore MS FRCS FRCS (ED)

Ingredients:

2 mangoes
1 yellow pepper - de-seeded and diced
A handful of lamb's lettuce leaves - washed
A handful of rocket leaves - washed
2 spring onions - trimmed and finely sliced
225 g (8 oz) dolcelatte - de-rind and sliced

For the dressing:
2 tablespoonfuls sunflower oil
2 tablespoonfuls hazelnut oil
1 tablespoonful white wine vinegar
1 teaspoonful Dijon mustard
Squeeze lime juice
salt and freshly ground black pepper

Method

Place a mango on the work-top and hold firm with the flat of your hand. Using a sharp knife, cut into the stalk end in a slightly upward direction so that the blade travels along the outside of the large flat central stone. Remove top half of the mango, then turn mango over and repeat with the other side. Peel and slice flesh. Prepare other mango in the same way. Place in a bowl with yellow pepper, lamb's lettuce, rocket and spring onions. Mix dressing ingredients and seasoning in a screw-top jar and drizzle over salad. Toss to coat and pile on to plates. Sit dolcelatte slices on top and finish with a twist of black pepper.

kipper cocktail

Dr J H Gilkes

Ingredients:

4 ozs kipper fillets
juice of ½ lemon
⅛ pt (70 ml) double cream
3 inches (7-8 cm) cucumber finely diced
pepper and salt
a few lettuce leaves
⅛ pt (70 ml) home-made or good commercial brand mayonnaise
a little cayenne pepper

Method:

Mince the kipper fillets, place in a basin and pour the lemon juice over. Leave to stand for a few minutes, stirring occasionally. Add cucumber and mix well. Mix cream with mayonnaise. Add other ingredients and season to taste. Stir well to ensure even blending. Place the lettuce leaves in individual pots and spoon out the mixture. Sprinkle a little cayenne pepper on the top.

gazpacho

Mr A J Woolf FRCS FRCOS

Ingredients:

2 small cloves of garlic
6 large ripe tomatoes
1 large green pepper
1 cucumber
1 Spanish onion
6 tablespoons lemon juice
salt
cayenne pepper
¾ pint (430 ml) tomato juice
3 level teaspoons butter
2 slices diced dried bread
1 ice cube
a little butter

Method:

Skin the garlic. Blend in a blender 4 tomatoes and 1 clove of garlic. Add ½ onion, 1/4 green pepper and ½ peeled cucumber, and blend again. Strain into serving dish and chill. Just before serving, blend together the olive oil, lemon juice, salt, pepper and tomato juice. Stir into the above mixture and add the ice cube. Chop the remaining vegetables, and put each vegetable into a separate bowl to accompany the soup. Fry diced bread and garlic in a little butter, and serve in a small bowl.

chicken liver pate

Dr Hawley

Ingredients: serves 6

3 oz (85 g) butter
8 oz (225 g) chicken liver
4 rashers streaky bacon, chopped
1 small onion
1 clove garlic
pinch of dried thyme
pinch of mixed spices
1 tablespoon cream
1 tablespoon sherry

Method:

Melt 1 oz (25 g) butter. Fry the chopped bacon and onion till soft, not brown. Chop the liver and cook briefly till firm but still pink. Add the crushed garlic. Cool slightly, then liquidise or mince. Add the cream, sherry, thyme, spice and 1 oz (25 g) butter. Tip into the dish. Melt the rest of the butter and pour over the pâté. Refrigerate. Can be served with French bread or toast.

pommes aligot

Dr B Solomons

Ingredients: serves 4

1 kg (1 ¼ lb) potatoes
100ml (3 ½ fl oz) milk
100 ml (3 ½ fl oz) crème fraiche
80 g (3 oz) butter
1 clove of garlic
500 g (18 oz) cheese (a young tomme de cantal is recommended, or eg wensleydale)
pepper and salt

Method:

Peel and boil the potatoes till cooked but firm (or 10 minutes in a pressure cooker).
Mash with the warm milk, cream, butter and crème fraiche, adding garlic, pepper
and salt. Put the purée into a thick-bottomed casserole and over a low heat mix in
the thinly sliced cheese, lifting the mixture well until it almost stands up when
dropped from the spoon.

sole and smoked salmon terrine

This recipe is included here with the kind permission of Ebury Press.

Mr Martin Bailey FRCS

Ingredients:

550g (1 ¼ lb) Dover or lemon sole fillets, skinned
15 ml (1tsp) lemon juice
2 egg whites
150 ml (¼ pint) double cream or fromage frais
175 g (6 oz) young spinach leaves, shredded
salt and pepper

For the smoked salmon cream:
175 g (6 oz) smoked salmon
1 egg white
75 ml (3 fl oz) crème or fromage fraiche or double cream
cayenne pepper
lemon juice
red and green peppers, thinly pared cucumber skin and lemon rind to garnish

Method:

Put the sole in a blender or food processor and blend to a purée. Add the lemon juice and salt and then the egg whites. For a really smooth terrine, pass the mixture through fine sieve. Return the purée to the blender or food processor and, with the motor running, very gradually pour in the cream or fromage frais. Season with pepper. Chill for at least 1 hour. Blend the smoked salmon to a purée. Add a squeeze of lemon juice and then the egg white. Pass through a fine sieve as for the sole, then return to the blender or food processor. With the motor running, gradually pour in the creme fraiche or cream. Season with cayenne pepper. Chill for about 1 hour. Cook the spinach with 15 ml (1tablespoon) water until wilted. Drain well, then rinse in cold running water. Drain well again, pressing down on the spinach to extract as much water as possible. Purée in a blender or food processor and season. For the garnish, grill the peppers until they are soft and the skins are charred all over. Allow to cool, then peel them. Discard the cores and seeds. Cut the peppers into decorative shapes and arrange with the cucumber skin and lemon rind on the bottom of a lightly oiled 25 x 10 cm (10 x 4 inch) terrine. Carefully cover the bottom and sides of the terrine with about two-thirds of the sole mixture. Leave an open channel in the centre.

Place about half of the smoked salmon mixture in the channel, then cover the salmon with the spinach purée. Cover with the remaining smoked salmon mixture and cover this with the remaining sole mixture. Cover the terrine with greased greaseproof paper. Put the terrine into a roasting tin. Surround with boiling water and bake at Gas Mark 3 (170 degrees C /325 degrees F) for about 50 minutes or until just set in the centre. Remove the terrine from the oven and leave to cool. Drain off any excess cooking liquid. Carefully unmould the terrine on to a cold plate. Garnish the plate with thinly pared strips of cucumber skin. This dish may be made the day before and chilled overnight.

oriental prawn

This dish can also be served as a light main course. It is nutritive and delicious.

Dr Mathew Johnson MB MRCGP

Ingredients:

1 ½ lb (680 g) fresh tiger prawns (not pre-cooked)
2 inches (5 cm) stem ginger
2 cloves garlic
5 tablespoons soya sauce (Japanese soya sauce is the best)
1 lime
2 green chillies

For the salad:
cucumbers, sliced
radishes, sliced
carrots, sliced
honey
sesame oil

Method:

Peel the prawns. Finely chop the stem ginger, garlic, and chillies. Put into a bowl and pour in the soya sauce. Add the juice of ½ a lime and marinate the prawns in this mixture for 45 minutes. Arrange the thinly sliced carrots, radishes and cucumbers around the perimeter of a serving dish. Make a dressing of one part each of lime juice, honey and sesame oil. Pour this over the arrangement. Grill the prawns under a high heat for 2 - 3 minutes per side. Place these cooked prawns in the middle of the serving dish and serve. If you wish to serve this as a main meal, then include some rice.

lamb's liver pate

This is a recipe given to me by a friend in South Africa - Bridget Gomm.

Lotte Darby

Ingredients:

1 kg (2 ¼ lb) lambs liver
2 cloves garlic - crushed
2 level teaspoons salt
250 ml (9 fl oz) cream
1 tablespoon Worcestershire Sauce
400 g (14 oz) butter
50 ml (2 fl oz) lemon juice
1 level teaspoon black pepper
100 ml (3 ½ fl oz) brandy
100 g (3 ½ oz) sliced almonds to garnish

Method:

Remove fibrous matter from the liver and cut up into small pieces. Fry the liver and garlic in half the butter. Add lemon juice and liquidise with remaining ingredients. Put in moulds - cover surface with melted butter. Chill and sprinkle with the nuts. The nuts can also be added to the pâté mixture if desired.

roquefort salad

Dr B Solomons

Ingredients:

150 ml (5 fl oz) roquefort cheese
75 ml 2 ½ fl oz) vinegar
juice of a lemon
1 level teaspoon dry mustard
125 ml (4 fl oz) olive oil
60 ml (2 fl oz) cream

Method:

Stir together the cheese with the vinegar. Add lemon juice, the mustard and —
gradually — the olive oil stirring vigorously. Add the cream, and mix.

main courses

cheese souffle with fillets of sole

Karen Leth

Ingredients:

4 egg yolks
5 egg whites
2 ½ oz (70 g) grated cheese - gruyère and parmesan in equal parts
salt & pepper to taste
1 oz (25 g) butter
4 fillets lemon sole

Method:

Roll up the fillets of sole, seasoned with salt and pepper and cook in a buttered dish in the oven for 5 minutes. They do not need to be quite cooked as they are to cook again in the soufflé. Butter a soufflé dish and place the fillets at the bottom, well drained of any liquid that comes from them while cooking. Separate the eggs. Beat the cheese into the yolks until the mixture is creamy. Whip the egg whites very stiffly and fold them into the yolks. Pour quickly into the soufflé dish and put straight into a pre-heated hot oven. Cook for 12 - 15 minutes.

chicken à la gilkes

Dr Gilkes

Ingredients:

1 chicken, quartered
2 tablespoons oil
3 pears, peeled, cored and sliced
1 small can prunes
1 red pepper
1 tablespoon flour
1 chicken stock cube
¼ pint white wine (dry)
¼ pint water
grated rind of one lemon

Method:

Strain the prunes and reserve the syrup. Sauté the chicken pieces in the oil until brown on both sides. Place in a casserole dish. Sauté the red pepper until just cooked and add to chicken with prunes and pear slices. Thicken the juices in the sauté pan with flour. Add chicken stock, white wine and half the prune juice and lemon rind. Pour over the chicken and cook in a covered casserole for one hour at 375 degrees F.

macaroni cheese and bacon

Dr C N Mallinson FRCP

Ingredients:

1 packet macaroni
2 medium sized onions
uncooked ham or bacon, the amount depending on taste
20g (¾ oz) butter to finish

For the batter mixture:
3 level tablespoons flour
½ pint (280 ml) milk
1 egg

Method:

Cook the macaroni in boiling water, drain and set aside. Fry the onions until golden brown and set aside. Whisk the flour gradually into the milk, add the salt and pepper and then beat in the egg. Take a large ovenproof dish which has been well buttered. Start with a layer of macaroni in the base of the dish, followed by layers of onions and bacon. Repeat these layers until the dish is full. Dot some butter on the top, pour in the batter mixture, which should come just below the top of the macaroni, and grate some hard cheese over the lot. Bake in a medium oven for 1-1½ hours until top is brown and crisp.

orange and tarragon chicken

Dr Edmondson

Ingredients:

1 ½ oz (40 g) butter
2 tablespoons oil
4 chicken breasts (each one divided into 3 pieces)
1 large onion
6 ¼ oz (180 g) frozen orange juice
¼ pt (140 ml) water
1 chicken stock cube
4 sprigs of fresh tarragon
½ oz (12 g) cornflour
5 oz (140 g) sour cream
parsley or tarragon to garnish

Method:

Brown chicken in the oil and butter and place in a warm dish. Cook the onions for 2 or 3 minutes. Stir in the orange juice, water, stock and chopped tarragon. Bring to the boil, stir and add the chicken and cook until tender (about 20 minutes). Blend the cornflour with 2 tablespoons of water and add carefully, stirring continuously for 2 or 3 minutes. Stir in the sour cream. Garnish with chopped parsley or tarragon.

pheasant in red wine

Mr H N Whitfield

Ingredients:

2 large pheasants, each cut into 4 pieces
4 ozs (115 g) green bacon
2 medium onions finely chopped
2 cloves garlic finely chopped
3 tablespoons butter
2 tablespoons oil
12 button mushrooms
1 pint (570 ml) red wine
1 tablespoon flour
bouquet garni
Salt and pepper to taste

Method:

Heat half of oil and 1 tablespoon of the butter in a large thick pan, sauté the bacon
cubes until golden and transfer to casserole. Add onions, garlic and mushrooms to
pan, sauté for a few minutes and add to casserole. Put the rest of the oil and butter
into the pan, sauté the pheasant until golden and add to the casserole. Pour the
red wine into the pan and combine with the juices. Cook on a high flame until
liquid is reduced by a third. Thicken with remaining butter and flour. Simmer for
a few minutes, strain into the bowl and allow to cool slightly so that any fat can be
skimmed off the surface. Adjust seasoning, pour into casserole, add the bouquet
garni and cook in a moderate oven until pheasant is tender.

chicken with almonds and raisins

Dr Edmondson

Ingredients:

6 level tablespoons blanched almonds
1 inch (2.5 cm) cube of fresh ginger,
coarsely chopped
1 inch (2.5 cm) stick of cinnamon
2 bay leav
5 cloves of garlic
6 tablespoons vegetable oil
6 chicken breasts (cut into pieces)
6 whole cardamon pods

5 whole cloves
1 level teaspoons salt
3 onions - peeled and finely chopped
2 teaspoons ground cumin
¼ level teaspoons garam masala
⅛ level teaspoons cayenne pepper
1-2 level tablespoons sultanas
½ pt (280 ml) single cream

Method:

Put the ginger, garlic, 4 level tablespoons almonds and water into blender and blend until it turns into a paste. Heat the oil in a large frying pan and brown the chicken pieces - remove and place in a warm dish. Add to the pan the cardamons, cinnamon, bay leaves and cloves. Fry for a few seconds. Add the onions - fry for 3 to 4 minutes until lightly brown. Add the paste from the blender, the cumin and cayenne - stir for 2 to 3 minutes until the oil separates from the mixture. Add a tablespoonful of the yoghurt and stir for 30 seconds. Now add the rest, a spoonful at a time, until all the yoghurt has been incorporated. Add the chicken pieces and any liquid that may have accumulated. Add the cream and salt. Cook over a low heat for 15 minutes. Add the sultanas and cook for a further 10 minutes. Stir in the garam masala. Garnish with roasted almonds.

honey glazed chicken

Dr Lewis Clein

Ingredients:

4 chicken quarters
2 tablespoonsolive oil
1 tablespoon clear honey
2 tablespoons Dijon mustard
2 level teaspoons curry paste or 1 tablespoon lemon juice

Method:

Put the chicken pieces, skin side up, in a roasting tin. Stir all the other ingredients together in a bowl and mix well. Spoon over the chicken and then cover with foil. Bake for half an hour at Gas Mark 4 (350 degrees Fahrenheit/175 degrees Celsius). Then remove the foil and bake for another half hour, basting the chicken with the mixture occasionally.

ginger and garlic leg of lamb with sherry sauce

Dr Gillian M Vanhegan MB BS DRCOG MIPM

Ingredients: serves 6

Leg of lamb
½ inch (12 mm) fresh root ginger
2 cloves garlic
1 teacup sherry
1 tablespoon soy sauce

Method:

Before roasting the leg of lamb, make pockets under the skin and fill with small slivers of fresh ginger and garlic. Make the gravy in your usual way using juices from the meat tin. Add a cup of medium dry sherry and a tablespoon of soy sauce to the gravy. Boil up and serve with the meat. Ratatouille is a good accompaniment to this dish.

noodles with cream and fresh herbs

Dr Sturridge

Ingredients:

1 lb (450 g) egg noodles, fresh if possible
½ pint (280 ml) cream
parsley
chives
rosemary
2 cloves garlic
4 oz (115 g) butter
salt and freshly ground pepper
parmesan, freshly grated

Method:

Warm the cream. Cook the noodles in boiling salted water until just tender but with a bite. Drain thoroughly. Chop the herbs together coarsely. Stir into the noodles the heated cream, half the butter, the pounded garlic and chopped herbs, and season with salt and plenty of ground pepper. Put a tablespoon of grated Parmesan on top of each plateful of noodles and a good knob of butter on top of that. A plate of these looks particularly good: creamy white with green herbs and a yellow pool of butter in the centre. As in all spaghetti recipes, this sauce can be used on any kind of pasta, but is best on the thinner, more delicate kinds: spaghetti, tagliatelle, linquine, etc.

gravad lax

A Swedish marinated salmon in a mustard and dill sauce

C Bernhardson-Lundquist

Ingredients:

1 kg (2.2 lb) lax (salmon) preferably the middle bit
1 large bunch of fresh dill
1 tablespoon sugar
1½ teaspoons crushed white pepper
1 tablespoon coarse salt

For the Sauce:
1 tablespoon Swedish mustard
1 teaspoon dark French mustard
1 tablespoon sugar
2 tablespoons vinegar
1 dl (4 fl oz) oil
finely chopped dill.

Method:

Scrape the salmon piece and dry it well — do not rinse it. Halve it along the backbone. Cut away all bones but leave the skin. Mix the sugar, salt and pepper. Rub this mixture into both fish halves. Put plenty of dill onto the insides of the salmon halves. Place one half onto a big plate with the meaty side upwards. Place the other half on top in such a way that the thin end is on top of the thick end of the other half. Cover with a plate. Put a weight on top. Leave the salmon in a cool place with the weight on for 24 hours. Turn it over a few times and add further fresh dill. Scrape away the spices and cut the salmon into 2 cm (¾ in) thick slices - off the skin. Put the slices on a cool serving dish and garnish with fresh dill branches. For the sauce, mix the mustard, sugar and vinegar. Add the oil slowly in a fine stream stirring vigorously. Finally, add plenty of dill.

pork in a cream and mushroom sauce

Dr John Coltart

Ingredients: serves 12

3 lbs (1.14 kg) diced pork
Mushroom sauce (see sauces) or, alternatively, use
3 cans of Campbells Cream of Mushroom Soup
3 green bell peppers
3 onions - chopped
½ lb (225 gm) mushrooms
3 cooking apples
3 teaspoons vinegar
3 teaspoons sugar
3 tablespoons flour
salt and pepper to taste
oil for frying
3 tablespoons cream
parsley for garnishing

Method:

Toss the diced pork in flour and fry in oil until brown. Remove from the oil and set aside. Remove the seeds from the bell peppers and slice thinly. Peel and slice the apples. Add the pork, peppers, onions, apples, sugar, salt and pepper to the mushroom sauce in a casserole dish and cook for 1 hour on Gas Mark 4 or 350 degrees F/175 degrees C. Add the sliced mushrooms ten minutes before the end of cooking. Garnish with cream and chopped parsley.

sauerbraten

Dr M Kellett

Ingredients:

1 cup red wine
1 tablespoonful wine vinegar
1 carrot, sliced
1 onion, sliced
3 cloves 1 bay leaf
½ teaspoon dried thyme
1 teaspoon dry mustard
6 peppercorns, crushed
1.5 Kg (3 lb) topside of beef
50 g (2 oz) lard or sunflower oil
2 tablespoons flour
1 cup (5 oz/140 gm carton) soured cream
½ cup stock or water
½ teaspoon salt

Method:

Combine the vegetables, wine, vinegar, salt and spices in a large bowl. Add the meat in one piece, cover and marinate in the refrigerator for at least 24 hours, turning three or four times. Before cooking, remove the meat, pat dry, and brown on all sides in hot lard or oil. Meanwhile bring the marinade to the boil. Simmer for 2-3 minutes, then pour it over the meat. Add water or stock to half way up the meat. Cover with foil and a tightly fitting lid and bake slowly in a medium oven for two hours. To serve, remove the meat, strain the sauce, mix the flour and the cream together and slowly dilute, stirring all the time, with some of the hot stock. Return to the pan and cook for a few minutes until the sauce has thickened. Taste for seasoning. Slice the meat on a serving plate and coat with the sauce or, if you prefer, serve the sauce separately. Serve with German Cucumber Salad (see starters) which should be placed in individual bowls as a side salad and a dish of potatoes boiled in their jackets.

roast lamb of pauillac

Jonathan Bradbeer

Ingredients:

2 ½ oz (70 g) stale bread, crusts trimmed
8 cloves of garlic
2 oz (50 g) butter
salt
freshly ground pepper
8 level tablespoons chopped flat leaf parsley
1 leg of lamb about 3 ½ - 4 lbs (1.6-1.8 kg), trimmed
2 tablespoons of peanut oil

Method:

Pre-heat the oven to Gas Mark 8 (450 degrees F/230 degrees C). Coarsely grind
the bread crumbs in a food processor. Finely chop 6 cloves of garlic and cut 2 into
slivers. In a bowl combine the butter, salt and pepper, bread crumbs, parsley and
chopped garlic. Mix to a smooth paste with a fork. Make slits in the lamb and
insert the garlic slivers using the point of a knife. Season lamb with salt and
pepper and spread with the garlic paste. Coat the lamb with the oil and season
with salt and pepper. Oil a large roasting tin and place the lamb on a rack in the
tin, rounded side down. Roast for 20 minutes, then turn it over. If part of the
paste comes off, gently press it back on; the rounded side is now upper most, and
this surface will be on display as the dish is carved. Reduce heat to Gas Mark 7
(425 degrees Fahrenheit/215 degrees Celsius). Check that the pan juices do not
burn — they should just caramelise. If they do burn, add some warm water a little
at a time. After 45 minutes of cooking, turn off the oven and let the lamb rest for
10 minutes in the oven. Serve in slices, sprinkle with the pan juices and serve.

mousaka

This traditional Greek dish comes from modified recipes of my older relatives in Cyprus who, in turn, obtained it from their mothers.

André Symeou BSc DipP PsyC

Ingredients: serves 4-6

Minced meat and sauce:
½ lb (225 g) extra lean minced pork*
½ lb (225 g) extra lean minced lamb*
1 medium onion, finely chopped
salt and pepper (black)
1 cup dry red wine
½ tablespoon tomato purée
juice of ½ lemon
1 large tomato, chopped
1 bunch of parsley, finely chopped
 (do not use ready chopped packets)
cinnamon (ground)
nutmeg (ground)
very light oil

*vegetarians can use Quorn

Vegetables:
2 large aubergine
2 large courgettes
3 large potatoes
very light oil
olive oil
3 level tablespoons bread crumbs
Béchamel sauce:
3 level tablespoons butter
5 level tablespoons flour
4 cups of milk (hot) & 1 cup double cream
½ cup grated cheese (halloumi is best)
salt and pepper
ground cinnamon
 nutmeg
pinch of baking soda

Method:

Initial Preparation:
Vegetables:
Peel the aubergines, courgettes and potatoes. Cut the aubergines into long thick slices, lay out on a tray and salt to remove bitterness. Leave for 15 minutes, dry and turn over, leave for another 15 minutes. Slice the courgettes and potatoes thinly, salt and fry them all separately in light oil mixed with a little olive oil until golden brown. Stack them on a strainer and press to extract the oil.

Minced Meat & Sauce:
Heat the minced meat gently in a frying pan for a few minutes and drain off water produced. Add some oil and the onions and season with salt and black pepper. Stir the mixture until the meat is light brown. Add the wine and boil for 2 minutes. Reduce heat and stir in tomato purée dissolved in lemon juice. Now add the chopped tomato and parsley. Keep stirring and add cinnamon and nutmeg generously. Lower the heat and continue cooking for about 15 minutes or until the liquid has been absorbed.

66

Béchamel Sauce:

The order here is important. Melt the butter in a pan and add 4 level tablespoons of sieved flour whilst stirring with a wooden spoon into a roux. Add gradually 4 cups of hot milk, stirring all the time with an egg whisk. Add salt, pepper and generous cinnamon and nutmeg. Remove from heat and mix in the whisked eggs. Return to the heat and add the cream. Stir in the cheese and thicken with 1 level tablespoon of sieved flour. Add a pinch of baking soda and increase the heat stirring all the time until it becomes a thick cream.

Final Preparation:

Sprinkle the base of an oven dish (10 x 8 x 3 inch/25 x 20 x 7.5 cm) with some bread crumbs and put in a layer of potatoes. Sprinkle with cheese, cinnamon and nut-meg, and add a layer of courgettes. Sprinkle again with cheese and spice. Then spread a little béchamel sauce over. Cover this with the minced meat mixture and sprinkle with cheese and spice. Add the aubergine layer, sprinkle again. Add the remaining potatoes now to cover, and press a little. Sprinkle again with cheese and spice and then cover generously with the thick béchamel sauce. Sprinkle once again lightly with cheese and spice and remaining bread crumbs. Cook in a medium oven for about 40 minutes.

Note:

Let the dish cool and then cut into squares. Serve hot or cold with a Greek salad. Often Moussaka is more delicious the next day. The following go very well with Moussaka:

Starter:

Dips: taramasalata, tachini, talattouri, warm pitta and green olives stored in olive oil, lemon, garlic & crushed coriander seeds.

Dessert:

Watermelon & Honey dew.

larry's lancashire chip butty

Dr L R I Baker MA MD FRCP FRCPE

Ingredients:

4 slices of white sandwich bread (avoid brown bread, granary, seeded or other 'healthy' varieties) per person.
butter (no margarine)
salt
vinegar
potatoes (waxy varieties)
cooking oil

Method:

Heat liberal quantities of oil in deep frying pan until spitting. Peel potatoes and cut into large broad chips, place in chip basket and lower into oil. Butter bread (liberally and right to the edges). Remove and drain chips when cooked (onto kitchen paper). Place chips between two slices bread, salt heavily, add vinegar to taste (until bread soggy in my case). Slice...eat.

marinated venison in bechamel sauce

Venison marinated in white wine and cognac served with Behamel sauce and wild rice.

Mr Geoffrey Longson

Ingredients:

3 lb (1.4 kg) roe venison (shoulder or haunch)
12 ozs (350 gm) butter
2 tablespoons oil
1 glass white wine
¼ pint (140 ml) cream
¼ pint (140 ml) béchamel sauce (see sauces)
2 tablespoons rich stock
juice of 1 lemon
1 glass cognac
2 bay leaves
salt and pepper

Marinade:
¼ pint (140 ml) olive oil
¾ pint (420 ml) red or white wine
1 onion
1 carrot
2 sticks celery
2 cloves garlic
6 peppercorns
6 juniper berries
1 bay leaf
parsley
thyme.

Method:

Chop all the vegetables and garlic for the marinade. Crack the peppercorns and mix all the ingredients together before submerging the meat. Marinade for at least 12 hours (up to three days for very old meat), turning the meat occasionally.

Melt the butter in a casserole with the oil and add the venison which has been cut into chunks. Brown the meat nicely all over, then add the wine and continue to cook over a lower heat for about one hour, stirring occasionally to prevent it sticking. Then stir in the cream, béchamel sauce and stock with the bay leaves and continue the cooking for another 10 minutes. Just before serving, add the lemon juice and cognac and adjust the seasoning. Serve very hot with wild rice.

poulet aux noisettes et framboises

Mr O A Gilmore FRCS

Ingredients: serves 6

3 chicken breasts - skinned and boned
6 rashers of bacon
1 teaspoon toasted sesame seeds

Stuffing:
1 dozen raspberries
1 tablespoon hazel nuts
2 sprigs of basil
3 button mushrooms
1 tablespoon Philadelphia cheese

Method:

Stuffing:
Combine hazelnuts, raspberries, mushrooms and basil. Chop the mixture coarsely and then mix with the Philadelphia cheese.

Chicken:
Flatten out the chicken breasts using a tenderiser. These should be twice the size once flattened. Spreading the stuffing on at one edge, roll the chicken into a sausage-like shape and hold together with the strips of bacon. Lastly, sprinkle with the sesame seeds. Bake for 15-20 minutes in a hot oven. To serve, cut the chicken rolls into half-inch (12 mm) rounds and serve.

gigot d'agneau en croute with gratin dauphinois

Jean Dalrymple

Ingredients:

1 leg of lamb up to 1 kg (2 ¼ lb)
3 lamb kidneys, diced
1 ½ oz (40 g) butter
armagnac brandy (a little)
4 oz (115 g) mushrooms, chopped
thyme
rosemary
tarragon
8 oz (225 g) puff pastry
3 eggs
2 lb (900 g) potatoes, peeled and thickly sliced
¾ pint (430 ml) milk
5-6 oz (140-170 g) grated cheese
garlic

Method:

Bone the meat as far as the shank so as to leave the bone as a handle. Fry the kidneys, mushrooms, thyme, rosemary and tarragon in butter, and stir in a little armagnac. Use this mixture to stuff the meat, sewing it up with kitchen thread. Roast for 2 hours at Gas Mark 4-5 (360 degrees F/180 degrees C), and let it cool. Roll out the puff pastry ½ inch (12 mm) thick and wrap the joint completely, moistening the edges of the pastry and pinching them together with the fingers. Brush with egg yolk and cook in a hot oven for a further 15-20 minutes. For the gratin dauphinois, peel the potatoes and cut into thick slices. Simmer in 3/4 pint (430 ml) milk until half cooked. Rub some garlic around a wide shallow oven dish. Beat up 2 eggs with 4 oz (115 g) of grated cheese and stir in the hot milk.Put the potatoes in the dish and pour the cheese custard over them. Top with the remainder of the grated cheese and brown in mid-oven at Gas Mark 4 (350 degrees F/175 degrees C) for 30-35 minutes.

duvenny pasta

Judith H Graham Secretary to Dr Blair

Ingredients:

1 lb (450 g) steak mince
1 tablespoon plain flour
2 onions - chopped
Garlic granules
½ lb (225 g) mushrooms - chopped
¼ pint (280 ml) Bovril cube stock
1 tin Campbell's mushroom soup
½ packet of pasta

Method:

Brown the mince in a little oil. Remove from heat and stir in flour. Add chopped onions, mushrooms and stock and bring to the boil, stirring continuously. Allow to simmer for about an hour. Add the mushroom soup and heat through. Meanwhile, cook as much pasta as you think you can eat. Mix pasta and mince and serve with a green salad.

swordfish with mustard-basil butter

This recipe is from the Churchill House Inn in Brandon, Vermont.

Dr H D Rowbotham

Ingredients: serves 4

¼ cup (½ stick) unsalted butter, room temperature
2 level tablespoons Dijon mustard
2 level tablespoons finely chopped fresh basil
vegetable oil
4 x 8 oz (225 g) swordfish steaks, ¾ inch (18 mm) thick
fresh basil sprigs

Method:

Mix the first 3 ingredients in a small bowl. Prepare barbecue or pre-heat the grill. Brush the grill with vegetable oil. Season the fish with salt and pepper. Grill the fish just until cooked through, about 3 minutes per side. Transfer to plates. Top each with a spoonful of mustard - basil butter. Garnish with basil sprigs and serve.

Alternative method (for swordfish or tuna):
Brush the steaks or fillets with a good oil and then season with garlic, salt and black pepper. Heat the griddle till it becomes dangerously hot, turn off the smoke alarm, throw on the fish steaks for about 2 minutes each side and then, just before presenting and whilst the fish is still on the griddle, squeeze over some lime juice. Smoke and steam fill the dining area and appetites are immediately engendered. Remember to turn the alarm back on after the smoke clears.

armenian lamb

Mr Michael Edgar

Ingredients:

2 lbs(900 g) fillet end of best leg of lamb or best neck fillets
1 tablespoon olive or vegetable oil
1 oz (25 g) butter
2 medium onions (sliced)
1 clove garlic (crushed)
1 oz (25 g) flour
1 level teaspoon ground cumin
½ level teaspoon ground allspice
2 tablespoons tomato purée
½ - ¾ pint (240-430) chicken stock
salt and pepper to taste

Method:

Cut the meat from the bone and divide into 2 inch (5 cm) squares. Heat the oil in a
metal casserole dish. Drop in the butter and, when foaming, brown the meat.
Remove the meat and place onto the casserole lid. Add onions and garlic. Cook
slowly for 5 minutes, stirring from time to time. Add the flour and spices, and
continue cooking for a further 3-4 minutes. Stir in the tomato purée and stock.
Blend till mixture is smooth. Add the meat and the juices. Cook in the oven at
Gas Mark 4 (350 degrees Fahrenheit/175 degrees Celsius). Serve with pilaff and a
green salad.

veal escalope a la creme

Mr Glyn Evans

Ingredients:

4 escalopes of veal
1 cup of white wine
½ cup plain flour
1 pint (570 ml) single cream
½ lb (225 g) mushrooms
2 cloves garlic
a few sprigs of parsley, chopped
salt and ground black pepper

Method:

Beat the escalopes of veal with a wooden hammer so that the veal becomes flat.
Coat the veal with plain flour. Half cook the veal with the white wine (about 1
minute). Put aside. Chop the mushrooms into fairly thick slices, place in a wok
and cover with water. Boil for about 3 minutes. Drain the mushrooms and
discard the water. Replace the mushrooms in the wok. Add some cooking oil, the
garlic, chopped parsley, salt and pepper. Cook until the mushrooms are crispy
and brown. Remove from the heat and add the single cream and continue cooking
on a low heat for about 3 more minutes. Place the veal with its juices of wine into
an ovenproof dish. Add the cream and mushroom sauce and cook in the oven on a
very low gas mark for about three quarters of an hour. Best served on a bed of
cooked rice.

poached sole & scallops in a mushroom sauce

Dr Alexander T D Williams

Ingredients: serves 4

8 medium sized lemon soles, skinned and filleted
8 plump scallops (in their shells)
1 oz (25 g) butter
¼ pint (140 ml) double cream
1 pint (560 ml) fish stock
½ (280 ml) pint dry white wine
1 oz (25 g) flour
½ lb (225 g) chopped mushrooms

Method:

Fold the sole fillets and place in a saucepan. Pour in fish stock. Place lid on saucepan and simmer for about six minutes until they are just cooked.

Lift out carefully and place on paper towels to dry before transferring to a serving dish. Keep warm. Remove scallops from their shells, clean well and dry with paper towels. Brush well with olive oil, and dust with salt. Place under the grill for one minute each side (or less, depending on size). Place them in the warming dish with the sole. Sauté the mushrooms in butter. Quickly boil the fish stock until it is reduced by about half. Add the wine. Soften the butter and gradually blend with the flour to make a paste. Gradually add into the stock whilst whisking gently. Reduce the heat and add the mushrooms. Simmer for 3 minutes and then add the cream, stirring continuously. Pour the sauce onto the sole and scallops. Serve with buttered new potatoes and peppered spinach.

chicken in mustard sauce

Dr J J Misiewicz FRCP

Ingredients:

medium sized chicken
2 dessertspoons of Worcestershire sauce
2 dessertspoons of Harvey's Sauce (obtainable from Harrods)
2 dessertspoons of mustard
pinch of cayenne pepper

Method:

Roast the chicken, cut up into parts, discarding the bones, and place in an ovenproof dish. Whip together the cream, Worcestershire Sauce, Harvey's Sauce, mustard and cayenne pepper. Pour over the chicken and place in a low oven until the sauce has melted over the chicken.

Cook's Notes: This dish is best served with plain rice and a green salad.

parmesan curried chicken

Mr Timothy ffytche FRCS

Ingredients:

1 small free-range chicken
2 heaped tablespoons flour
1 heaped tablespoon freshly grated parmesan cheese
1 level teaspoon salt
½ level teaspoon of medium Madras curry powder
1 small cup of water
2-3 tablespoons single cream

Method:

Joint and divide the chicken into 12 pieces and coat each piece in the flour mixture. Pre-heat oven on Gas Mark 6 (400 degrees F/205 degrees C). Prepare shallow baking tin with small amount of sunflower oil. Place chicken pieces skin-side down in a baking dish in a single layer and bake uncovered for 20 minutes, then turn pieces and bake for a further 25-30 minutes until skin is crisp and brown. Place on a bed of plain rice on a large platter. For the sauce, add the flour mixture to the juices remaining in the baking tin. Cook over a low heat, slowly stirring in a small cup of water and 2-3 tablespoons of single cream to make a thick sauce. Season further with curry powder and salt as required. Serve with a chicory and mandarin salad with pine kernels.

mrs kirkham's macaroni and cheese pudding

Dr Kirkham

Ingredients:

12 oz (340g) macaroni
1 pint (570 ml) milk
2 oz (50g) butter
12 oz (340 g) mature cheddar cheese
2 tablespoons flour
salt and pepper to taste
1 level teaspoon English mustard powder or
2 level teaspoons English made mustard

Method:

Boil the macaroni in salted water for 20 minutes. Drain and put back in the pan.
Add 1/4 pint (140 ml) of milk, all the butter, 8 oz (225g) grated cheese. Make a
paste with the flour, the rest of the milk, salt, pepper and mustard, and add to the
macaroni. Cook till it thickens and then put it into a buttered baking dish. Cover
with the rest of the grated cheese. Put in a slow oven (Gas Mark 2/310 degrees F/
155 degrees C) for 45 minutes until brown and crispy on top.

pork pie

Dr Sturridge

Ingredients: serves 6-8

1 lb (450 g) lean end of belly of pork or blade
salt and freshly ground pepper
water
dried sage
½ pint (280 ml) stock
½ teaspoon gelatine

For the pastry:
12 oz (350 g) plain flour
pinch salt
4 oz (115 g) lard
¼ pint (140 ml) water
1 egg yolk (for glaze)

Method:

Trim the meat, mince half of it as finely as you can and chop the other half into pea-sized pieces; it takes a long time. Season well, add sage to your liking and moisten with half a wineglass of water. Pre-heat the oven to Gas Mark 8 (450 degrees F/230 degrees C). To make the pie-crust, sift the flour with the salt and put to keep warm in a large bowl. Melt the lard, cut in pieces, in the water in a small saucepan, and then bring to the boil; as it boils pour it on to the flour. Mix rapidly with a wooden spoon until it is smooth. Reserve a quarter of the pastry for the lid, keeping it warm. Flatten out the rest as soon as it is cool enough to handle. When it is about quarter to half an inch (6-12 mm) thick, mould it into a pie shape on the bottom of a large greased jam or storage-jar. Lift it, jar and all, on to a greased baking tin, wait until the crust is cool, and gently ease the jar away. It may collapse a bit, but never mind. You should have a case about five inches (12-13 cm) in diameter and two or three inches (5-7.5 cm) high. Fill the case with the meat, pressing it down well; roll out a lid from the last piece of pastry and damp the edges with water before sealing it on very carefully. With your fingers, press the edges together and decorate them by indenting with the back of a knife at half-inch (1 cm) intervals or by forking. You can decorate the pie with pastry trimmings cut into leaves and flowers. Tie a band of oiled greaseproof paper round the pie. Paint the top with egg yolk, and make a round hole in the middle for the steam to escape and to pour the juice through.

Bake in the centre of a hot oven for half an hour and then turn the heat down to Gas Mark 5/375 degrees Fahrenheit/190 degrees Celsius and cook for another hour. Remove the pie and allow it to cool a little. Strain the pig's foot stock and reduce to about ⅓ pint (190 ml). Season with salt, take it off the heat. Put the gelatine in a jug and add the stock. Stir and allow to cool a little. Fill the pie with this liquid, using a small funnel. Let it set and keep the pie overnight if possible. Eat it cold.

fleischpfanne mit kase

Mr Roger Burr FRCS

Ingredients:

2 onions
2 tablespoons oil
400 g (14 oz) pork fillet
200 g (7 oz) magerer gekochter schinken
(honey roast ham is the nearest equivalent)
1 red pepper (optional)
salt, pepper
400 g (14 oz) gouda cheese

Method:

All the ingredients should be thinly sliced including the gouda cheese. Fry the onions in oil until soft, add the pork, schinken, seasoning and red pepper if used, and fry until meat is cooked. Put cheese slices in a layer over the surface. Put lid on the frying pan and leave for 3-4 minutes to let the cheese melt. This is good served with fresh watercress covered in a French dressing.

gnocchi with bacon mushrooms and pesto sauce

Dr L A Price MD MRCP

Ingredients:

6 oz (170 g) pasta shells
½ lb (225 g) lean back bacon
½ lb (225 g) mushrooms - chopped
1/4 pt (140 ml) double cream
3 tablespoons green pesto sauce
2 tablespoons olive oil
knob of butter
black olives, chopped peppers and/or grated cheese as accompaniment

Method:

Boil the pasta in salted water with a few drops of olive oil added to it to prevent sticking; follow the directions on the packet. Put oil and butter in a large non-stick frying pan. Cut the bacon into small pieces with scissors and fry gently for about 5 minutes. Add the chopped mushrooms and fry for a further minute. Drain the pasta and add to the frying pan. Pour the cream over. Add the pesto sauce, mix together and serve immediately. If necessary, serve with separate side dishes of pitted black olives, chopped peppers and grated cheese.

loin of pork with herbs

Dr Lloyd

Ingredients:

a boned loin of pork
2 tablespoons mixed herbs
2 tablespoons lard
salt
pepper
1 ¼ kg (2 ½lb) small potatoes

Method:

Knead the herbs into the lard, and season. Score the rind of the pork into diamonds and coat the joint with the herb paste, keeping some of it aside. This will be spread into the gaps in the skin as they open up during the cooking. Weigh the joint and place it on a trivet in an oven pan. Parboil the potatoes in their skins, peel them and arrange them whole around the joint in the pan. Put into a cold oven and heat to 200 degrees C/400 degrees F/Gas Mark 6. Cook at 25 minutes per pound (55 minutes per kilogram), turning the joint occasionally so that the rind crisps all round. When this has been done, cover the pan with aluminium foil, reduce the heat if necessary and let the joint cook through. Check progress with a long fine skewer; when withdrawn, the point should be at the same temperature as the part near the surface. To serve, remove the crackling and carve the joint as for a leg of lamb. Those who like garlic can stick cloves into the meat before cooking: two will be quite sufficient.

steak pie

Mr Michael A Smith

Ingredients:

1 ½ lb (680 g) frying steak
1 onion, chopped
Oxo cube
½ pint beef stock
puff pastry
flour
oil
1 egg yolk

Method:

Trim the steak and cut into cubes. Dust with flour, add the onion and stir fry in oil. Braise in a low oven for an hour. Add stock and the Oxo cube, and place the mixture in a pie dish. Roll out the pastry to cover the dish. Brush with beaten egg yolk, and place in a hot oven until the pastry is browned.

provencal beef stew

This is a wonderful informal dinner party casserole from France.

Mr Patrick James

Ingredients:

2 lb (900 g) chuck steak
1 lb (450 g) onions
2 tomatoes, peeled and sliced
1 carrot, sliced
2 tablespoons olive oil
1 wine glass of red wine
a few sprigs of thyme
salt and pepper to taste
4 oz (115 g) black olives

Method:

Cook the sliced onions in the olive oil. Do not allow them to brown. Add the beef in one piece and cook until the beef is browned on each side. Add the tomatoes, carrot, thyme and seasoning. Pour the wine over the meat. Cover the pan and cook gently in the oven at Gas Mark 2-3 (325 degrees F/165 degrees C, for 4 hours. Add olives before serving.

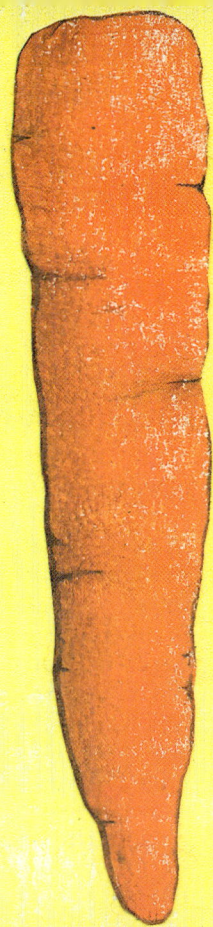

braised oxtail with garden vegetables

This recipe is by Anton Mosimann. My family and I have always enjoyed it very much.

Dr Louis Hughes

Ingredients:

16 pieces oxtail, well trimmed
Salt and freshly ground pepper
20g (¾ oz) plain flour
50 ml (2 fl oz) vegetable oil
20g (¾ oz) butter
100 ml (4 fl oz) red wine
2.5 litres (4 ½ pints) brown beef stock
150g (5 oz) mixed onion, carrot and celery very finely diced
½ garlic clove, finely chopped
50g (2 oz) diced tomato
1 bay leaf
2 sprigs thyme

For the Garnish:
50g (2 oz) each of carrot, swede and turnip, turned and blanched
50g (2 oz) button onions, peeled and blanched
25g (1 oz) small mangetout
25g (1 oz) butter
15g (½) oz parsley, finely chopped

Method:

Season the oxtail, and dust with the flour. Heat the oil in a large frying pan, and brown the oxtail well. Remove from the pan and set aside. Clean pan gently with kitchen paper. Add the butter, onion, carrot, celery and garlic to the pan and saute lightly. Pour in the red wine and deglaze the pan. Transfer into a suitably large, heavy saucepan. Add the diced tomato and the oxtail. Add 500 ml of the stock (18 fl oz) to the pan, and reduce to a caramel. Repeat once more then add the stock to cover the oxtail. Add the bay leaf and thyme and simmer for 2 ½ -3 hours, or until the meat is tender. Add more stock as necessary. Remove oxtail from sauce and discard the vegetables and herbs. Strain the sauce, bring to the boil, and skim until all grease is removed. Put the oxtail back into the sauce and place in a dish. Heat the garnish vegetables through in a pan with the butter, season and spoon over the oxtail. Sprinkle the parsley over the meat, and vegetables and serve.

cold chicken with rice

Mr John Sheperd

Ingredients:

1 large chicken, cooked, cooled, boned and cubed
1 green pepper, diced
3 ½ oz (100 g) rice
½ pint (280 ml) stock
⅛ pint (70 ml) orange juice
1 tablespoon olive oil
½ level teaspoon oregano
½ level teaspoon thyme
seasoning to taste

Garnish:
4 white grapes
blanched almonds
grated rind of an orange
1 tablespoon olive oil
½ tablespoon white wine vinegar

Dressing:
⅛ pint (70 ml) mayonnaise
2 tablespoons white wine vinegar
½ tablespoon olive oil

Method:

Mix the dressing, mix and add the cubed chicken, peppers, oregano, thyme and seasoning and set aside. Soak the rind in the oil and vinegar and leave for the flavour to diffuse. Cook the rice with the stock and orange juice (see appendix for details on cooking rice). Arrange the cooked rice to form a ring on a serving dish and garnish with the rind. Pile the chicken mixture in the middle and finish by scattering the grapes and blanched almonds. This dish can be prepared the day before, and is a wonderful addition to a buffet table.

good friday fish pie

Mr M A R Freeman MD FRCS

Ingredients:

2 lbs (1.8 kg) fish - boneless
(cod or haddock, for example)
salt and pepper
1 bay leaf
½ pint (280 ml) water or white wine
2 oz (50g) butter
2 oz (50 g) flour
¾ pt (430 ml) stock
asparagus tips or peas or both
1 level tablespoon fresh tarragon
(or ½ level teaspoon dried)
good pinch of nutmeg
6 ozs (170 g) peeled prawns, mussels or both (cooked)
3 tablespoons double cream

Topping:
2 oz (50 g) butter
4 oz (115 g) fresh white breadcrumbs
2 oz (50 g) chopped hazelnuts
2 oz (50 g) grated cheddar cheese

Method:

Place fish in a buttered ovenproof dish. Season with salt and pepper. Add the bayleaf, and water or white wine. Cover with foil and bake in a pre-heated oven at Gas Mark 2-3 (320 degrees F/160 degrees C) for approximately 25 minutes. Flake the fish and reserve the liquid. Melt butter, add the flour and cook for a minute or two. Gradually add the milk and ¼ pint (140 ml) of the reserved juice from the fish. Stir well and bring to the boil. Cook until smooth and thickened. Remove from the heat and add cooked asparagus or peas, tarragon, nutmeg, salt and pepper. Fold in the prawns, mussels or both and add the cream. Spoon into the buttered dish. To make the topping: Melt the butter in a heavy bottomed pan. Add the bread crumbs; stir until golden. Remove from the heat; stir in the hazelnuts and the cheese. Sprinkle over the fish mixture. Place under a pre-heated grill for about 2 minutes. Serve with salad or green vegetables.

spinach filled cannelloni

Ingredients:

1 oz (25 g) butter
1 oz (25 g) flour
7 fl oz (200 ml) milk
grated cheddar cheese
salt, pepper and freshly grated nutmeg
8 oz (225 g) frozen spinach - allow to thaw
8 oz (225 g) cottage cheese
cannelloni tubes (about 8)
butter for greasing
parmesan (optional)
4 oz (115 g) mushrooms (optional)

Method:
Melt butter, stir in flour and milk then cheddar cheese to make a smooth cheese
sauce. Season with the salt, pepper and nutmeg. Place the spinach in a bowl, mix
in the cottage cheese and the seasoning. Stuff the cannelloni tubes with either a
teaspoon or a piping bag. Place stuffed tubes in a greased dish, cover with sauce
into which you may add sliced mushrooms. Cover with sprinkling of freshly
grated parmesan and cook in pre-heated oven at Gas Mark 5 (375 degrees F/190
degrees C) for about ½ hour until cooked and browned. Serves 2 people. Excellent
for vegetarian guests or for a light lunch served with a green salad.

chicken and orange salad

John & Alison Shepherd

Ingredients:

1 cooked chicken
1 green pepper
mixed herbs
grapes
blanched almonds
3 ½ oz (100 g) rice
½ pt (280 ml) stock
⅛ pt (70 ml) orange juice

⅛ pt (70ml) mayonnaise
2 tablespoons white wine
½ tablespoons olive oil
2 oranges
1 tbs olive oil
½ tablespoon white wine vinegar
orange peel

Method:

Use the peel grated off the 2 oranges and mix with the olive oil and vinegar. Set aside. Cook the rice in the stock and orange juice until soft — it takes about 15 minutes. Leave to cool and then form a ring around the edge of the serving dish with the rice, leaving a space in the centre. Sprinkle the peel to decorate carefully on top of the rice. Cut up the chicken into cubes, saving a little of the breast to decorate on top. Add the chopped green pepper, herbs, mayonnaise, white wine and olive oil. Put this mixture into the centre of the dish so that the rice is all around it. Garnish with grapes, almonds, orange segments and the breast of the chicken.

desserts

chocolate toronne

Dr Sarkany

Ingredients: serves 8 to 10

¼ lb (115g) plain block of chocolate
2 tablespoons rum
¼ lb (115 g) unsalted butter
1 oz (25 g) castor sugar
1 egg yolk
2 ½ oz (70 g) ground almonds
1 egg white
pinch of salt
3 oz (85 g) marie biscuits.

Method:

Grease a 7 inch (18 cm) round sandwich tin. Break the chocolate into small pieces and place in a saucepan with the rum. Melt over a very gentle heat. Remove the saucepan from the heat before the chocolate has fully dissolved. Allow to cool slightly. Cream the butter and sugar till light and fluffy. Add egg yolk, beating well. Fold in ground almonds then the melted chocolate. Beat egg white and salt till stiff and standing in peaks. Fold egg white into creamed mixture. Break biscuits into small pieces and fold into the mixture. Pour into prepared cake tin. Allow to set overnight in the refrigerator. Slip a knife around the edge of the cake and carefully turn out onto a plate. Decorate with cream if liked.

amaretti delight

Dr David Darby

Ingredients:

amaretti biscuits
raspberries - fresh or frozen
whipped cream
liqueur, white wine or sherry
flaked almonds (optional)

Method:

Roughly break up some Amaretti biscuits and put in the bottom of a glass, serving dish, or individual dishes. Sprinkle with Amaretti di Sarona liqueur or white wine or sherry. Cover with raspberries. Top with lashings of whipped cream and flaked almonds if liked.

yoghurt whip

Mr H N Whitfield

Ingredients:

8-10 fl oz (230-280 ml) whipping cream
8-10 fl ozs (230-280 ml) Greek yoghurt
2 tablespoons amaretto liqueur (optional)
soft brown sugar

Method:

Whisk the cream with the amaretto until thick, carefully fold in the yoghurt and turn into a serving dish. Sprinkle the top heavily with the brown sugar and leave for up to 24 hours so that the sugar turns into a sauce and it all sets slightly.

chestnut cake

Karen Leth

Ingredients:

2 ½ lbs (1.15 kg) chestnuts
¼ pint (140 ml) milk
2 oz (50 g) sugar
1 oz (25 g) brandy
6 eggs
Caramel:
½ oz (15 g) sugar
3 tablespoons water

Method:

Roast the chestnuts for 20 minutes in a slow oven so that both the shells and skins peel easily. Finish cooking them in boiling water. Strain the chestnuts and then purée them by passing through a sieve. Add the milk, sugar and brandy to the puree. To prepare the caramel, boil the water and sugar till thick and golden. Coat the bottom and sides of a cake tin with it. Pour in the chestnut mixture and cook it in a moderate oven for 1 hour. Remove from oven and leave to cool. Then turn it out and serve with cream.

strawberries and mint with lemon syllabub

A delicious combination of fresh summer strawberries and mint, topped with a spoonful of creamy lemon syllabub.

Dr Lloyd

Ingredients:

450 g (1lb) strawberries, cleaned and quartered
1 level teaspoon freshly chopped mint
1 level tablespoon castor sugar

Syllabub:
½ lemon, grated rind and juice
3 tablespoons sparkling grape juice or orange juice
40 g (1 ½ oz) castor sugar
150 ml (¼ pint) double cream
fresh mint sprigs to decorate

Method:

Mix together the strawberries, mint and sugar in a bowl to marinate. Meanwhile, place the lemon rind and juice, grape or orange juice and castor sugar in a bowl. Slowly whisk in the double cream until the mixture stands in soft peaks.

Divide the strawberries and any juice that has been drawn out by the sugar between 6 dessert glasses and top each with a large spoonful of the lemon syllabub. Decorate with a sprig of fresh mint.

Not suitable for freezing.

tiramsu

Dr Andrew Griffiths

Ingredients:

2 eggs (size 2 or 3)
6 oz (170 g) castor sugar
6 fluid oz (170 ml) strong black coffee
1 carton mascarpone
1 packet sponge finger biscuits
1 tablespoon Tia Maria or kirsch - optional

Method:

Separate the eggs. Beat the egg whites until they form soft peaks. Mix together the mascarpone, egg yolks and sugar. Mix together the coffee and liqueur (if used). Dip biscuits into the coffee mixture and arrange in a layer in a bowl. Spoon over some mascarpone mixture. Continue to fill the bowl with alternate layers of biscuits and mascarpone. Finish with a layer of mascarpone. Refrigerate for 2 hours.

cheesecake

Mr Philip Starr

Ingredients:

7/8 digestive biscuits, crushed
1 ½ lbs (680 g) curd cheese
1 cup granulated sugar
2 eggs
2 large cartons sour cream

Method:

Heat oven to Gas Mark 4-5 (360 degrees F/180 degrees C) . Place crushed biscuits in base of greased 8 inch (20 cm) loose-bottomed tin. Beat together cheese, eggs and sugar for about 5 minutes. Add 1 carton of sour cream and beat 30 seconds more. Pour mixture on top of biscuits. Bake for 30 minutes. Remove from oven. Mix 1 tablespoon of sugar into the second carton of sour cream and pour this on top of the cake. Return to oven for 5 minutes only. Remove and allow to cool. May be decorated with tinned mandarins, pineapple pieces, fresh peach slices or strawberries.

lemon and brandy syllabub

Dr J J Misiewicz

Ingredients:

zest of 1 Lemon
juice of 1 lemon
⅛ th (70ml) pint brandy
3 oz. (85 g) castor sugar
½ pint (280 ml) double cream
¼ pint (140 ml) sweet white wine

Method:

Combine the lemon zest and juice in a jug. Add the brandy and leave overnight, if possible. Strain through a sieve the following day. Add the castor sugar and stir until dissolved. Add the double cream and wine. Whip until solid. Add the lemon peel to decorate.

forecast's chocolate cake

Dr D Forecast

Ingredients:

<u>Sponge Mixture:</u>
10 oz (285 g) self-raising flour
8 oz (225 g) Castor sugar
1.5 level teaspoons baking powder
7 oz (200 g) mayonnaise
4 level tablespoons cocoa
8 fl oz (225 ml) boiling water
1 teaspoon vanilla essence

<u>Icing:</u>
2 level teaspoons instant coffee
2 level tablespoons cocoa
2 tablespoons hot water
3 oz (85 g) margarine
8 oz (225 g) icing sugar

Method:

Mix the self-raising flour, castor sugar, baking powder and mayonnaise together. Pour the boiling water over the cocoa and vanilla essence, mix and add to the flour mixture. Place in a greased soufflé dish and bake at Gas Mark 4 (350 degrees F./ 180 degrees C) for 1¼ hours. For the icing, mix the coffee, cocoa and hot water together and set aside. Mix the margarine and icing sugar together and add to the coffee mixture. Use this mixture to ice the cake all over and leave to mature for at least 2 days.

welsh cakes

Angela Mills

Ingredients:

2 oz (50 g) cooking fat
2 oz (50 g) margarine
4 oz (115 g) sugar
8 oz (225 g) flour
3 oz (85 g) mixed fruit
1 egg
a little milk, if necessary
1 level teaspoon mixed spice
rind of 1 lemon

Method:

Place the flour and sugar in a mixing bowl and rub the fat into the mixture. Add the remainder of the ingredients and mix into a light, soft pastry. Roll out ¼ inch (6 mm) deep and cut into biscuit shapes. Cook on a medium heat in a lightly oiled frying pan, preferably a cast-iron one, for about 15 minutes or until cooked.

orange ice cream

Dr Edmondson

Ingredients:

6 egg yolks
8 oz (85 g) castor sugar
rind and juice of 2 oranges and 1 lemon
½ pint (280 g) double cream
fruit for filling (kiwi, fresh peaches, etc)

Method:

Beat the egg yolks and sugar until creamy. Add the rind and juice of the oranges and lemon. Whip cream until just holding, and add to egg mixture. Pour into a ring-mould, cover and freeze. Turn out when required and fill the centre with choice of fruit.

michael's chocolate delight

This is a delicious pudding/non-cook cake which can be made days in advance, as it keeps for up to two weeks in the refrigerator if the cream is omitted.

Dr Michael Newton MD FRCP

Ingredients:

2 egg yolks
2 egg whites
6 oz (170 g) icing sugar
2 tablespoonfuls double cream
2 tablespoonfuls kirsch or brandy
3 oz (85 g) flaked butter
6-8 ozs (170-225 g) dark chocolate
4 ozs (100 g) finely crushed petit beurre or osborne biscuits
a few peeled grapes or a handful of dried fruit

Method:

Add butter and sugar to melted chocolate and stir. Add the cream, raw beaten egg yolks, kirsch or brandy and mix well. Fold in the stiffly beaten egg whites. Place the mixture in a shallow cake tin with well oiled paper or removable bottom. Store in the refrigerator overnight. Turn out onto a plate and decorate with whipped cream, grapes and nuts.

Cook's Note: If making this for a buffet supper, it is worth slightly increasing the amount of crushed biscuits so that it has a firmer consistency and is not so gooey.

chocolate hazelnut cake

Professor Linda M Luxon

Ingredients: serves 8

100g (4oz) self raising flour
pinch of salt
225 g (8oz) unsalted butter, softened
225 g (8 oz) light soft brown sugar
4 eggs, separated
100 g (4 oz) shelled hazelnuts, finely ground
225 g (8 oz) plain chocolate, grated

To finish:
300 ml (½ pint) double cream
50 g (2 oz) hazelnuts, roughly chopped
175 g (6 oz) plain chocolate, broken
into pieces
100 g (4 oz) icing sugar, sifted
4 tablespoons water

Method:

Oven: 170 degrees C, 325 degrees F, Gas Mark 3. This cake can be made ahead of timeand stored in an airtight tin for a few days as required. It should not be assembled with the cream and frosting until just before serving, however, as the cream will not keep. For a cake that is less rich, the cream may be omitted and the cake simply served plain with the frosting and nuts on top — this would be more suitable for a tea-time cake rather than a dinner party dessert. Line the bottom of a greased 23 cm / 9 inch deep cake tin with non-stick parchment paper. Sift together the flour and salt and set aside.

Put the butter and sugar in a bowl and beat together until light and fluffy. Beat in the egg yolks one at a time, adding a little of the flour after each addition. Fold in the remaining flour, and then the hazelnuts and chocolate. Stir until evenly blended.

115

Beat the egg whites until stiff, then fold into the cake mixture. Spoon into the prepared tin and level the top. Bake in a pre-heated oven for 1 hour 15 minutes or until a skewer inserted in the centre of the cake comes out clean. Remove from the oven and leave to cool in the cake tin.

Turn the cake out of the tin and carefully peel off the parchment paper. Slice the cake in two.

To finish: whip the cream until it holds its shape, then spread over one half of the cake. Sprinkle with half the chopped nuts and place the other half of the cake on top. Stand the cake on a serving plate.

Put the chocolate, icing sugar and water in a heatproof bowl standing over a pan of gently simmering water and heat gently until the chocolate has melted, stirring constantly with a wooden spoon. Spread the icing immediately over the top of the cake with a palette-knife, then sprinkle with the remaining chopped nuts. Serve as soon as possible.

charleston apple cake

Mr Robert Morgan

Ingredients:

1 cup vegetable oil
2 eggs
2 cups sugar
2 cups self raising flour
3 bramley apples, thinly sliced
1 cup pecan nuts
3 level teaspoons ground cinnamon
2 teaspoons vanilla essence

Method:

Grease a flour tube pan, ie a high-sided round cake tin with funnel. Mix all the ingredients together and spread evenly into the pan. Bake for an hour at Gas Mark 4 (350 degrees F/175 degrees C).

orange and lemon cake

This recipe is very popular on our fishing picnics.

Dr Darby (Lotte Darby)

Ingredients:

6 oz (170 g) butter
6 oz (170 g) castor sugar
3 eggs
6 oz (170 g) self-raising flour
grated zest of 1 lemon and 1 orange
2 tablespoons orange juice

<u>Icing:</u>
2 oz (50 g) butter
6 oz 9170 g) icing sugar

Method:

Cream the butter and the sugar until light and fluffy. Add the beaten eggs and two-thirds of the zest. Fold in the flour and mix in two-thirds of the juice. Bake in two seven-inch (18 cm) tins for approximately 20 minutes at Gas Mark 4-5 (350 - 375 degrees F/175-190 degrees C). When cool, sandwich together with half of the butter icing made from 2 oz (50 g) butter and 6 oz (170 g) icing sugar plus the remainder of the zest and juice and top with remainder.

the rowbotham carrot cake

Dr Rowbotham

Ingredients:

2 cups plain flour
2 level teaspoons baking powder
2 level teaspoons ground cinnamon (1 level teaspoon for a less sharp taste)
4 eggs
2 cups sugar
1 level teaspoon salt
3 cups grated carrot
1 ½ cups oil
4 oz (115 g) walnuts (optional)

Icing:
2 oz (50 g) butter
4 oz (115 g) Philadelphia cream cheese
8 oz (225 g) icing sugar

Method:

Put the dry ingredients in a mixer, add the oil and mix for two minutes. Add the eggs and mix them in, followed by the carrots and — if you like — the walnuts. Bake for 30-40 minutes at Gas Mark 4 (350 degrees F/175 degrees C).

For the icing, melt the butter and remove from the heat. Add the cheese, mixing well until smooth.Now add the sugar gradually and beat until smooth.

nesselrode pudding

Dr B Solomons

Ingredients:

120 g (4 oz) mixed sultanas and raisins
120 g (4 oz) orange and lemon peel and glacé cherries
250 ml (9 fl oz) marsala
150 g (5 ½ oz) chestnuts
500 ml (18 fl oz) milk
570 ml (1 pint) double cream
5 egg yolks
150 g (5 ½ oz) sugar
vanilla essence
100 ml (3 ½ fl oz) cherry brandy or maraschino
marrons glacés

Method:

Soak the sultanas, raisins, peel and cherries in marsala for a few hours. Make a crème anglaise (custard) with the eggs, sugar and milk. Put the chestnuts through a mouli and stir into the custard with the vanilla essence. When the custard is cool add fruit and marsala, pour all into a ring mould and freeze. Remove from fridge 15 minutes from serving. Invert the mould onto a dish and cover with a hot damp cloth for a few minutes to detach the pudding from the mould. Serve surrounded with marrons glacés.

caramel fried fruits in cointreau

Dr James Griffiths

Ingredients:

bananas
nectarines
oranges
blackberries
strawberries
kiwi
butter
sugar
cointreau
cream or strained Greek yoghurt

Method:

Fry sliced fruit in hot butter until browned - no more; add sugar, and when caramelised stir in generous measures of Cointreau. Serve immediately from the frying pan with the cream or yoghurt.

raspberry pavlova

Jonathan Bradbeer

Ingredients:

1 lb (450 g) raspberries
3 egg whites
6 oz (170 g) castor sugar
¼ - ½ pint (140-280 ml) whipped cream

Method:

Whisk the egg whites until stiff and then whisk in half of the sugar, until egg whites are stiff once more. With a metal spoon, gently fold in the remaining sugar. Using a forcing bag, pipe into 2 large rounds drawn on a piece of greaseproof paper or baking parchment which has been lightly oiled. Bake at Gas Mark 1/2 (265 degrees F/130 degrees C) until firm, but not browned. When cool, remove from paper and store in an airtight tin until required. To prepare for eating, spread one round with half of the whipped cream and half of the raspberries. Place the second round on top and cover with cream and more raspberries. Decorate with fresh mint leaves. It is best assembled at the last moment, otherwise the meringue can go a little soft or chewy. If one round looks not as nice as the other, use that one for the base.

bramble ice cream

Mr Harvey White

Ingredients:

4 egg whites
4 egg yolks
4 oz (115 g) castor sugar
½ pint (280 ml) whipping cream
1 lb (450 g) puréed and sieved blackberries
2 ½ pint (1 L) container

Method:

Whip whites with sugar until very stiff, add yolks and cream. Finally add fruit and mix gently. It doesn't matter if there is a slightly marbled effect. Cover and freeze overnight.

chocolate coffee refrigerator slice

Dr and Mrs Geoffrey Guy

Ingredients: serves 6-8

30 ml (2 level tablespoons) instant coffee
46 ml (3 tablespoons) brandy
125 g (4 oz) plain chocolate
125 g (4 oz) English butter, softened
50 g (2 oz) icing sugar
2 egg yolks
300 ml (10 fl oz) fresh whipping cream
50 g (2 oz) chopped almonds, toasted
about 30 boudoirs (sponge fingers)

Method:

Make up the coffee granules with 200 ml (7 fl oz) boiling water and stir in the brandy; cool. Break up the chocolate and melt in a small basin with 15 ml (1 tablespoon) water; cool. Whisk the butter and icing sugar together until pale and fluffy. Add the egg yolks, beating well. Stir in the cool chocolate. Whip the fresh cream until softly stiff and stir half into the chocolate mixture with the nuts. Refrigerate the remaining fresh cream. Butter and base-line a 21.5 x 11.5 cm (8 1/2 x 4 1/2 inch) top measurement loaf tin with non-stick paper and line the bottom with sponge fingers, cutting to fit if necessary. Spoon over one-third of the coffee mixture. Layer up the tin with the chocolate mixture and sponge fingers soaking each layer with coffee, ending up with soaked sponge fingers. Weight down lightly and refrigerate for several hours. Turn out on to a serving dish. Decorate with remaining fresh whipped cream.

quick and easy butterscotch pie

Delicious served with vanilla ice cream

Dr Brian Pigott

Ingredients:

3 oz butter
6 oz granulated sugar
3 tablespoons double cream
½ teaspoon vanilla essence

Method:

Line a 7 ½ inch flan tin or pie plate with shortcrust pastry and bake blind; let it cool. Melt all the ingredients in a non-stick saucepan very slowly, stirring all the time. Bring to the boil and simmer for 5 minutes, stirring constantly. Pour into cold pastry case and allow to set.

mum's mush

This is a wonderful and very simple pudding and quantities can be added or subtracted to taste.

M H Ornstein FRCS

Ingredients: serves 4

1 sponge cake or 8 trifle sponges (stale is better as it is less crumbly)
1 level tablespoon raspberry jam
1 large tin pineapple pieces
3 tablespoons sweet sherry or port
2 oz (50 g) sultanas
2 oz (50 g) walnuts (optional)
double cream

Method:

Break up sponge and place in bottom of ovenproof dish. Mix in the raspberry jam.
Add the pineapple and juice, wine, sultanas and nuts. Mix gently. Cover and
place in oven on a low setting for half an hour until warmed through but not hot.
Serve in individual dishes covered with cream.

belgian loaf

An easy cake that is delicious on its own or spread with butter.

Dr John McKendrick

Ingredients:

1 cup sugar
1 cup milk
1 cup sultanas
4 oz (100 g) margarine
2 cups self-raising flour
pinch of baking soda
1 large egg

Method:

Bring the sugar, milk, sultanas and margarine to the boil in a saucepan and then leave to cool. Sieve in the flour and soda and add the beaten egg. Pour into 2 small bread tins which have been lined with greaseproof paper and cook at Gas Mark 5 (375 degrees F/190 degrees C) for 45 minutes.

zabaglione

Dr Gillian M Vanhegan MB BS DRCOG MIPM

Ingredients: serves 6

4 egg yolks
4 tablespoons castor sugar
4 tablespoons marsala wine
6 almond biscuits

Method:

Whip all the ingredients, except the biscuits, together in a pyrex bowl over hot water. The mixture will become very light and frothy. Pour it straight away into wine glasses and serve with the almond biscuits.

cocktails

sloe gin

Mr Harvey White

Ingredients:

4 lbs (1.8 kg) sugar
1 lb (450 g) sloes
1 bottle (700 ml) gin

Method:

Prick sloes and cover with sugar and gin. Shake daily at first, and then leave to steep for 3 - 6 months.

pharaoh shapiro

Dr Brian Kaplan MBBCh MFHom

Ingredients:

percolated or brewed coffee (not instant)
Häagen Dasz vanilla ice cream
Irish whiskey
creme de curaçao
Terry's chocolate orange
ice

Method:

Brew some good quality coffee, allow it to cool and then put it in the fridge until it is cold. Put into a blender one measure of Irish whiskey, one measure of Creme de Curacao, two or three cubes of ice, a couple of scoops of ice cream and about half a cup of coffee.

Garnish glasses with a single piece of Terry's chocolate orange. This is done by cutting a slit into each piece of the chocolate with a very sharp knife or scalpel which has been heated over the gas stove. Serve with a thick, short straw.

peach screech

Dr Peter Ryan

Ingredients: serves 5 - 10, depending

12 peaches
2 cups sugar
1 litre (1 ¾ pints) orange juice
1 bottle of good brandy
6 bottles of champagne

Method:

Peel the peaches, cut in half and remove and discard the stones. Place, hollow side up, in a large earthenware or stainless steel dish. Cover them very liberally with sugar and then drench them in freshly squeezed orange juice so that the peaches are completely covered. Leave for a few days or a week, depending on the weather, to ferment and then pour over them a bottle of good brandy. Just before drinking, pour in six bottles of champagne which need not be the very best. Stir gently so as not to lose all the bubbles, strain and drink.

blue lagoon

Ellen Parsons

Ingredients:

Curacao
1 bottle champagne

Method:

Mix enough Curacao with the chilled champagne to impart a blue colour. This is a wonderful drink for a party with a blue theme.

black velvet

Mr. John Simpson

Ingredients:

Equal parts of champagne and Guinness

Method:

Mix the Guinness and champagne and serve.

bucks fizz

Ingredients:

Equal parts of champagne and orange juice

Method:

Mix the chilled champagne and orange juice and serve.

appendix

pesto sauce

Ingredients:

4 oz (115 g) fresh basil
1 clove of garlic
14 tablespoons olive oil
2 oz (50 g) grated parmesan
salt and pepper to taste

Method:

Place all but the parmesan in a blender and blend to a smooth paste. Remove from the blender and stir in the parmesan. Serve.

mayonnaise

This can be bought ready-made in many supermarkets, but we have included this recipe for those who wish to make their own.

Ingredients:

2 large egg yolks
270 ml (½ pint) very light olive oil — do not use the extra virgin variety
lemon juice or whitewine vinegar
seasoning

Method:

Place the eggyolks in a mixing bowl and whisk. Add a couple of drops of oil and whisk. Continue to add the oil in a very thin but steady stream, whisking vigorously all the time. Stop pouring occasionally as you whisk to ensure that the oil is fully absorbed before adding any more. You will notice that the mayonnaise will start to thicken when about 50 ml (2 fl oz) of the oil has been incorporated. When all the oil has been whisked in, add about a tablespoon of lemon juice or vinegar and whisk again. Finally, add some salt. It can keep for about 48 hours if refrigerated.

Extra virgin olive oil is not advisable here as it will not only impart a green but will also make the mayonnaise taste rather bitter. Other oils may be substituted for the traditional olive oil, and herbs or garlic may be added to the finished sauce for variety.

white sauce

Ingredients:

1 pint (560 ml) milk or the strained milk from the recipe for béchamel sauce
1 ½ oz (40 g) plain flour
2 ½ oz (70 9) butter

Method:

Place the flour in a small bowl. Mix the milk with the flour a teaspoonful at a time until a thick paste is achieved. Then slowly add some more milk until the mixture becomes quite liquid. Pour the remaining milk into a saucepan and add the mixture to this. Stir and then heat gently whilst stirring vigorously with a wooden spoon or whisk to prevent lumps from forming as the sauce thickens. Should you find that the sauce is thickening too quickly and lumps are beginning to form, remove from the heat for about a minute and whisk the mixture vigorously. Then replace on a very low heat until cooked. Finally, add the butter and stir before using. The sauce should be ready in about 6 minutes.

chicken stock

Ingredients:

1 small chicken carcass or 4 chicken wings
2 pints (1120 ml) water
2 carrots
1 onion
1 turnip
1 celery stick
bouguet garni
1 cup white wine
1 bayleaf
2 sprigs of fresh or 1 level tablespoon oregano
salt and pepper

Method:

Chop the carrots and celery into chunks, halve the turnip and onion and place in a pan with the bouquet garni, bay leaf, oregano, wine, chicken carcass and water. Add the salt and pepper. Bring to the boil and then reduce the heat. Cover and let simmer for 3 hours. Strain the stock and, when it is cool, skim off and discard the congealed fat. The stock will keep in the refrigerator for up to a week. If a strong-flavoured stock is required, then an extra onion should first be finely chopped and fried with some butter and the chicken carcass or wings until brown. This should then be mixed with the water, wine and other ingredients mentioned above.

fish stock

This is not a traditional stock, but it does add a light and tantalising flavour to fish dishes.

Ingredients:

the head of a salmon, or any fish trimmings of an equivalent weight (ask your fishmonger)
1 ½ pints (850 ml) water
2 cups white wine
1 cup dry sherry
3 sprigs chervil
3 sprigs parsley
the rind of ½ lime
1 tablespoon lime juice
3 shallots
1 bay leaf
3 peppercorns
a few sprigs thyme

Method:

Place all the ingredients in a pan. Bring to the boil, reduce the heat and simmer for 3 hours. Strain and refrigerate until you need to use it.

vegetable stock

Ingredients:

2 pints (1.2 L) water
2 carrots
2 onions
1 - 3 cloves of garlic, whole
1 turnip
1 parsnip
1 celery stick
1 cup dry sherry
3 sprigs of parsley
3 sprigs of tarragon

1 large bay leaf
1 tablespoon dried oregano
1 tablespoon dried marjoram
a few sprigs of thyme and coriander
1 tablespoon cumin seeds
1 tablespoon dried dill or 3 sprigs of fresh dill
4 peppercorns
1 tablespoon dried fenugreek
butter for frying or a little vegetable oil

Method
Finely chop 1 onion and the garlic. Fry in the butter or vegetable oil until brown,
but do not allow to burn. Chop the carrots, 1 onion, turnip, parsnip and celery
stick coarsely. Place in a pan, add the fried garlic and onion, sherry, parsley,
tarragon, bay leaf, cumin seeds, oregano, marjoram, thyme, coriander, peppercorns, water and fenugreek and bring to the boil. Cover the pan with the lid,
reduce heat and simmer very gently for 4 hours. Strain and refrigerate the liquid
until ready for use. Will keep for up to one week.

beef stock

Ingredients

11b (450 g)stewing steak or one ox tail or bone
2 pints (1.2L)water
bay leaf
3 sprigs of parsley
2 onions
2 carrots
1 stick celery
1 turnip
1 parsnip
2 cups red wine (optional - for added richness)

Method

Coarsely chop the onions, carrots, celery, turnip and parsnip. Place in a sauce pan
with the bay leaf, water, wine and beef bone, stewing steak or ox tail. Bring to the
boil. Cover, reduce the heat and simmer for 4 hours. Let cool, skim the fat off the
surface, strain and refrigerate the liquid until you need to use it.

sauce vinaigrette

Ingredients:

1 teaspoon Dijon mustard
1 teaspoon lemon juice
2 tablespoon red wine vinegar (the white wine version can be substituted, but this is more tart in flavour)
1 teaspoon herb pepper (obtainable from the Safeway supermarkets or Selfridges)
5 tablespoon extra virgin olive oil

Method:

Mix the above ingredients. For a more substantial flavour, mix in a bottle and retain so that all the flavours will develop before use, but remember to shake the bottle before doing so.

cooked rice

Ingredients:

175 g (6 oz) rice per person
Water to cover the rice
salt

Method:

Bring the salted water to the boil in a pan. Add the rice, cover the pan and simmer
gently for about 15 minutes. Taste a few grains of the rice to ensure that it is
cooked before serving.

Wild Rice
The cooking procedure for this is the same as for rice, but boil for 30 minutes,
checking after 20 minutes.

Persian Rice
Basmati rice must be used in this recipe. This is a method of cooking in which
steam rather than water is used to cook the rice. As a consequence, the grains
remain separated. Place the rice in a bowl and rinse with water while swishing the

rice around. Empty the water and repeat until the water runs clear. This will remove some of the surface starch which will otherwise cause the grains to stick together. Boil the salted water and add the rice. Allow to boil for about 3 minutes and then remove and drain. Rinse the rice under the cold water tap to remove some more of the starch and set aside. Place about one cup of water and about 3 tablespoonfuls of butter in a pan and bring to the boil on a high heat. Transfer the rice to this pan in a pyramid shaped pile. Cover with the lid which has been wrapped in a kitchen cloth to absorb the condensation. After about 3-5 minutes, lower the heat to the minimum amount and allow the rice to cook for about 30 - 40 minutes, tasting a few grains to see if it is cooked. Place some butter, 1/2 cup water and salt in a small pan, bring to the boil and sprinkle this over the rice after about 15 minutes during the cooking time.

poached salmon

Ingredients:

2 salmon fillets
1 bay leaf
water
salt and pepper

Method

Place the salmon in a saucepan. Cover with water, add the salt, pepper and bay leaf. Bring to the boil and simmer gently for 15 - 20 minutes. Remove the salmon and allow the water to drain

mushroom soup

Ingredients:
½ 1b mushrooms, chopped
4 shallots, finely chopped
1 pint vegetable stock
** oz single cream**
salt and pepper
butter for frying

Method:

Fry the shallots in the butter until golden brown. Add the mushrooms and cook for a further 15 minutes. Add the vegetable stock, salt and pepper, bring to the boil and then lower the heat and simmer for 30 minutes. Remove from the heat and place the contents in a blender and blend into a thick soup. Alternatively, pass the mushrooms through a sieve and add to the preserved liquid. Add the cream, re-heat and serve.

bechamel sauce

Contributed by Mr. Geoffrey Longson of Harley Street to accompany his recipe for the Marinated Venison which appears in this book. The sauce can, obviously, be used for any recipe calling for bechamel sauce.

Ingredients:

½ pint (275 ml) milk plus a little extra
1 small onion
1 small carrot
1 stick celery - chopped
1 sprig parsley
few white peppercorns
1 oz butter
1 oz flour
salt and pepper

Method:

Pour half pint milk into the pan, add the onion, carrot, celery, parsley and pepper-corns. Bring the milk just to boiling point, stir well so you blend the other ingredients with the milk. Cover the pan, remove from the heat and allow to stand for about 1 hour. Strain the milk into a jug, add more milk if necessary to make the half pint again. Use to make white sauce.

mushroom sauce

Ingredients:

½ lb mushrooms
5 shallots
3oz butter
flour
½ pint vegetable stock

Method:

Finely chop the mushrooms and the shallots. Fry in the oil. Add the vegetable stock and blend in a blender. Re-heat.

Index

Amaretti Delight 101
Armenian Lamb 76
Bacon and Mushroom Quiche 34
Baked Vegetables 30
Belgian Loaf 131
Black Velvet 140
Blue Lagoon 139
Boned Loin of Pork with Herbs 87
Braised Oxtail with Garden Herbs 92
Bramble Ice Cream 127
Butterscotch Pie, Quick and Easy 129
Caramel Fried Fruits in Cointreau 122
Champ 32
Cheesecake 107
Charleston Apple Cake 117
Cheese Soufflé with Fillets of Sole 49
Chestnut Cake 103
Chicken a la Gilkes 68
Chicken and Orange Salad 97
Chicken in a Mustard Sauce 80
Chicken Liver Pâté 38
Chicken Pâté
Chicken with Almonds and Raisins 56
Chocolate Coffee Refrigerator Slice 128
Chocolate Hazelnut Gâteau115
Chocolate Toronne 100
Cold Chicken and Rice 94
Coquilles St. Jacques au Beurre Blanc 31
Courgette & Almond Soup 13

Creamy Chicken Pasta
Cullen Skink   23
Dolcelatte Salad with Mango 35
Duvenny Pasta 73
Easy Peasy Tomato Soup 33
Fleischpfanne Mit Käse 85
Gazpacho 37
Gigot d'Agneau en Croute 72
Gnocchi (Pasta with Mushrooms and Pesto Sauce) 87
Good Friday Fish Pie   94
Gravad Lax-Salmon   61
Grilled Goat's Cheese with Bacon and Walnuts 28
Guacamole 26
Hedgehogs 14
Honey Glazed Chicken 57
Kipper Cocktail 36
Lambs Liver Pâté 44
Lamb with Ginger, Garlic and a Sherry Sauce
Larry's Lancashire Chip Butty à la Harley Street 68
Lee's Potatoes 27
Lemon and Brandy Syllabub 108
Macaroni and Cheese Pudding 51
Marinated Venison Cooked in White Wine & Cognac 69
Michael's Chocolate Delight 114
Moussaka 66
Mum's Mush 130
Nesselrode Pudding 121
Noodles with Bacon, Garlic 50
Orange & Lemon Cake 118
Orange & Tarragon Chicken 53
Orange Ice Cream 113
Oriental Prawns 43
Parmesan Curried Chicken 81

Peach Screech 138
Pharaoh Shapiro 137
Pheasant in Red Wine 55
Pitta Pizza 19
Poached Sole with Scallops in a Mushroom Cream Sauce 78
Pommes Aligot 39
Pork Served in a Cream and Mushroom Sauce 62
Poulet aux Noisettes et Framboises 70
Provençal Beef Stew 90
Raspberry Pavlova 125
Roast Lamb Pauillac 65
Roquefort Salad 45
Rowbotham Carrot Cake 120
Salmon & Avocado Terrine 16
Salmon Mousse 11
Sauerbraten 64
Scampi with Pernod 10
Shrimps in a Lemon, Tomato & Peanut Sauce 21
Sloe Gin 136
Smoked Salmon Pâté 18
Sole and Smoked Salmon Terrine 40
Spinach Filled Cannelloni 96
Steak Pie 89
Strawberry, Mint, Lemon Syllabub 104
Sunny Chicken Salad 15
Swordfish with Mustard-Basil Butter 74
Tiramisu 106
Veal Escalope à la Crème 77
Welsh Cake 111
Welsh Soup 24
Yogurt Whip 102
Zabaglione 132